I would like to express my sincere appreciation to the many people who so willingly encouraged and helped me with ideas and suggestions. This book could not have been written without them.

EDUCATIONAL ENTERPRISES

Practical Guides for Education

Copyright 1993 by Educational Enterprises, P.O. Box 1836, Spring Valley, California 91979. All rights reserved. No part of this book may be reproduced by any means, transmitted, or translated into a machine language without written permission from the author/publisher. Printed in the United States of America.

ISBN 0-9636749-0-0

How to Get the Teaching Position You Want!

A Comprehensive Guide for the Teacher Candidate's Job Search

M. Phyllis Murton

How to Get the Teaching Position You Want!

is designed for

- ***ANYONE APPLYING FOR A FIRST TEACHING POSITION***

- ***THE TEACHER PREPARING TO MAKE A CHANGE***

- ***BRINGING YOUR CLASSROOM EXPERIENCE UP TO DATE***

- ***LEARNING HOW TO BE A SUCCESSFUL TEACHING CANDIDATE***

- ***LEARNING HOW TO GET THAT SPECIAL TEACHING POSITION YOU WANT***

TABLE OF CONTENTS

The Cover Letter 1

The Resumé 4

The Application 13

Preparing for the Interview 25

The Interview 29

Interview Questions

    Early Admittance to Kindergarten 31

    Elementary School Level 36

    Middle School Level 45

    High School Level 54

    High School Level Questions in Academic Areas .61

    Special Day Teacher 68

    Bilingual Teacher 74

    Post-Interview Follow-Up Techniques 79

Using Substitute Teaching to Get Started 81

A Superintendent's Perspective 84

A Principal's Perspective 89

Comments from a Counselor 93

Suggested Reading List 95

Additional Copies 97

INTRODUCTION

This book is designed to assist the person who is ready to apply for a first teaching position, the teacher who is currently teaching and is preparing to make a change to a different school, level, or subject area, and for the teacher who has been away from the classroom for awhile and would like to return. Educational issues change, new ideas and methods emerge, and what really takes place in the classroom varies as children bring fragments of our ever-changing world with them into our schools.

How to Get the Teaching Position You Want! provides essential information that will prepare, reinforce, and present the teacher candidate as a person who is knowledgeable and current in the field of education.

With the exception of the names of the district superintendent, the principal, the counselor, and some of the school districts, the names, addresses, and telephone numbers contained herein are fictitious.

THE COVER LETTER

The cover letter is the employer's first look at you as a potential employee. Not only must the letter be error free, but the form must appear professional, it must be easy to read, and your message must be clearly stated.

The body of your letter should include the following: a statement of the position for which you are applying, a reference to the particular school district, a brief account of why you believe you are a qualified candidate, a sentence that says you are enclosing your resumé, and, if possible an application, and a closing line that communicates your desire for an interview. The tone of your cover letter should be sincere, positive, and enthusiastic.

The following examples, one for a beginning teacher and one for an experienced teacher, illustrate the above requirements and go one step further by presenting each teacher candidate as a caring person. This additional asset is both appealing and necessary for success in the classroom.

COVER LETTER SAMPLE 1

Michael J. Edwards
9357 Larkspur Street
Del Mar, California 92014
(619) 755-3911

Date

Samuel T. Jones
Director of Certificated Personnel
Encinitas Union School District
189 Union Street
Encinitas, California 92014

Dear Dr. Jones:

I am happy to hear that you will soon be interviewing teachers who wish to teach at the elementary level. It is with anticipation that I look forward to sharing my interest in high quality education with the Encinitas Union School District.

My multicultural student teaching experiences, the two years I spent as a Teacher's Assistant, my year as a camp counselor, my many special interests and varied work background have all strengthened my desire to work with children. Successes in these areas have encouraged the wish to become a teacher who can make a difference. I am enclosing a resumé that includes further details and qualifications.

I look forward to hearing from you in regard to scheduling an interview. Thank you for your consideration.

Respectfully,

Michael J. Edwards

COVER LETTER SAMPLE 2

Charlotte M. Dawson
1234 Broadway
Cardiff, California 92007
(619) 632-7755

                                                               Date

Julie M. Edmonton
Director of Personnel
ABC School District
University City, California 92000

Dear Dr. Edmonton:

I am delighted to hear that you will soon be interviewing teachers for positions in your district at the secondary level. I am applying to the ABC School District, because I have a strong desire to become an integral part of this community. The importance placed on quality education in your district creates an atmosphere in which I would like to teach and raise my family.

My eight years of teaching business and home economics classes have provided many opportunities for success on both an academic and a personal level with my students. Successes outside of the classroom include developing and implementing an advanced computer course, updating the home economics courses to conform to district standards and the state framework, and serving as a Department Leader for five years. I am enclosing a resumé that includes further details and qualifications.

I look forward to hearing from you in regard to scheduling an interview. Thank you for your consideration.

Respectfully,

Charlotte M. Dawson

THE RESUMÉ

When you send a resumé to a potential employer, the resume is representing you in your absence. It can not be emphasized strongly enough that your resumé must be perfect. It must be well-organized, contain no errors, and, while presenting all important information, it should leave the reader wanting to know more about you. This will lead to the interview you want, giving you a chance to talk with the employer, and demonstrate who and what you really are!

The following basic resumé form was described to me by a district superintendent as "dynamite." Included are three sample resumés: one for a beginning teacher, one for a teacher with minimal experience, and one for an experienced teacher.

The paper you choose for your resumé should be twenty-five percent cotton or "resumé" paper, as it is sometimes called. The paper ought to be white or a very light cream color. The weight and color of your paper will represent you as a professional person.

It has been said that the average resumé receives approximately thirty seconds of someone's attention In my opinion, unless there are unusual circumstances, your resumé should never exceed two pages (the following samples are longer due to page size). The size of the printed letters (12 points except for your name, which is 14 and in bold print), the form, and the spacing between items determine readability. Ease of readability often determines how much information is transferred from the paper to the reader in a very short time. Make your resumé count!

RESUMÉ SAMPLE 1

Janice L. Warren
1252 Larkspur Street
El Cajon, California 92020
(619) 449-5209

EDUCATION   Thirty-eight graduate quarter units, Teacher Credentialing Program to be completed January, 1993, University of California, San Diego

B.A., English, San Diego State University, California, December, 1991

CREDENTIAL   California Single Subject Credential - English, to be awarded January, 1993

STUDENT TEACHING EXPERIENCE   Grossmont High School, Grossmont Union High School District, El Cajon, California, September, 1992 - January, 1993

This assignment included a ninth grade English college preparatory class and an eleventh grade English class comprised of remedial and special education students. In both multicultural classes I developed and implemented literature and writing units, using cooperative learning groups, outside speakers, and people from the community. My principal interest is in using literature as a catalyst for personal growth and the building of self-esteem. I was responsible for parent conferences, participated in Parent Night, and helped supervise the Dance Club.

San Diego High School, San Diego Unified School District, San Diego, California, Summer, 1992

The tenth, eleventh, and twelfth graders in my summer school class had all failed their English classes. My goal was to reach them in a way that they would trust me enough to believe that with effort they could learn the required material and reach their goals. I taught by having students speak through controversial, critical thinking questions developed from the literature.

Muirlands Middle School, San Diego Unified School District, San Diego, California, March and April, 1992

In this multicultural seventh grade English class, I taught literature, working with individual students and with students in groups. I was able to be a part of the mock United Nations project in which the district participates.

RELATED EXPERIENCE	Volunteer parent in varying grade levels at the elementary level---extensive experience as a story teller, 1981 - 1986
	Presenter of adult seminars on self-esteem, developed and wrote the material in booklet form, 1979 - 1981
COMMUNITY SERVICE	Board of Old Town Community Theater, 1983 - 1985 Involved in youth theater productions
	Taught Sunday School at the high school level, 1980 - 1983
HONORS AND AWARDS	Scholarship, Soroptomist Club, January, 1992
	Scholarship, Department of Education, University of California, San Diego, June, 1992
MEMBERSHIPS	Golden Key Honor Society, San Diego State University, Member as of January, 1991 National Council of Teachers of English, 1992
SPECIAL SKILLS AND INTERESTS	IBM, Word Perfect, travel (traveled to Europe five times, Israel, Canada, Mexico), theater, jazz, opera, all music, ballroom dancing
REFERENCES	Furnished upon request

RESUMÉ SAMPLE 2

Catherine A. Smith
5291 Jansen Street
La Mesa, California 91941
(619) 270-6683

EDUCATION Special Education and Computer classes, 30 units, University of San Diego, California, 1988 through the present

Math, 1983 - 1985; Music, General Education, 1970 - 1971, 45 units, Mesa College, San Diego, California

Drama, 1982 -1983, nine units, San Diego State University, San Diego, California

Bachelor of Arts, Music, Scripps College, Claremont, California 1971 - 1975

CREDENTIAL Multiple Subject Elementary Education, June, 1989; Clear - January, 1990; Supplementary authorization in music, Grades six through nine

TEACHING EXPERIENCE <u>Elementary School Teacher - Half-time, Spring, 1990, to the present</u>
San Diego Unified School District, San Diego, California, Rolando Park Elementary School

I currently teach a multicultural group of 24 fourth graders with a wide range of backgrounds and abilities. My class performed a rap and Christmas song at our Winter Program; my *a cappella* singing group also performed. I was a part of developing and writing the Single Site Plan in Language Arts and am the Language Arts Representative for grades three through five. In addition, I tutored third, fourth, and fifth graders one hour daily in language arts and math.

Rolando Park Elementary School, Spring Semester, 1990

I was hired under VEEP to teach reading to second through fifth graders who were reading below grade level. This included whole language experiences, using literature to expand vocabulary, readers' theater, writing process, choral reading, oral presentations, discussions, and the use of computers for lesson extensions, creative writing, tutorials, and rewards. I also had the opportunity to work out the Visual and Performing Arts Component of Self-Study for PQR.

<u>Substitute Teacher - Half-Time, Spring, 1990 to the present</u>, Rolando Park Elementary School, Grades Second, Third, and Fourth

STUDENT TEACHING EXPERIENCE

La Mesa /Spring Valley School District, La Mesa, California

La Mesa Dale Elementary School, February - June, 1989

I taught a multi-cultural group of third and fourth graders in a team-teaching situation; gained experience in preparing and implementing lesson plans for all subjects, clinical teaching, writing-based lessons, hands-on techniques (manipulatives and crafts), writing and administering of tests, and use of music dramatization (with costumes) and visualization to intensify the learning experience.

Practicum Student, September - December, 1988

I worked with a multi-cultural group of first and second graders in reading; gained experience in CAP testing program; used multi-cultural literature, basal readers, helped with student journals; taught phonics; wrote and performed original music on a synthesizer to enhance literature lessons. I taught multicultural groups of fourth and fifth graders; time was divided between GATE and regular classes; gained experience in tutoring math, spelling, reading, language arts, and library skills.

RELATED EXPERIENCE	Piano Teacher, 1976 - 1988
	Voice Teacher, 1979 - 1985
COMMUNITY SERVICE	First Unitarian Church of San Diego Accompanist and co-director of Children's Choir, 1990 - 1991
	Accompanist for Family Theater Production, 1982
SPECIAL SKILLS	Apple IIGS, piano, guitar, singing
REFERENCES	Furnished upon request

RESUMÉ SAMPLE 3

Robert A. Carlson
2240 Lemon Avenue
Chula Vista, California 91913
(619) 634-7925

EDUCATION   M.A., Counseling, University of San Diego, San Diego, California, 1984

B.A., Physical Education, San Diego State University, San Diego, California, 1982

A.A., Grossmont College, El Cajon, California, 1980

CREDENTIAL   California Single Subject Credential, K - 12, 1984

TEACHING EXPERIENCE   <u>Elementary School Teacher, September, 1987 through June, 1988</u>

Rio Linda Union School District, Rio Linda, California
Blake Elementary School

In this teaching experience I taught kindergarten and first grade children in a self-contained classroom I instructed small groups of migrant children, grades kindergarten through third, led parent meetings, served as the school site representative to the Superintendent's Council and Professional Improvement Committee, communicated staff concerns to District Superintendent, and served as a member and secretary to the district School Site Council.

<u>Elementary School Teacher, September, 1989, through June, 1992</u>

Monrovia Unified School District, Monrovia, California, Mayflower Elementary School

This multicultural teaching experience included fifth and sixth grade students in a bilingual program. I used small cooperative learning groups to teach all subjects, developed and implemented several units designed to strengthen basic skills, and created an immensely successful positive reward system of behavioral management. I served as a Team Leader, as advisor to the sixth grade council, served on a district Language Arts committee, and participated in sixth grade camp.

RELATED TEACHING EXPERIENCE

Y.M.C.A., El Monte, California, July and August, 1989 - 1991

Assistant Program Director for Day Camp, working with physical fitness and nutrition program. I also supervised outings.

St. James House, Rio Lindo, Califrornia, July and August, 1986 - 1988

Senior Supervisor for the day camp for children, ages six through thirteen, planning and facilitating all activities, such as crafts, art, cooking classes, songs, games, sports, and outings.

COMMUNITY SERVICE

Summer Camp Counselor and Art Assistant, 1981 - 1982

Rio Lindo Summer Recreation Program, 1983 - 1985

SPECIAL SKILLS AND INTERESTS

IBM, Word Perfect, guitar, camping, backpacking environmental concerns, member of Greenpeace, jazz, dancing, theater

REFERENCES

Furnished upon request

THE APPLICATION

When you send your application to a potential employer, as with the resumé, the application is representing you. It must be <u>perfect</u>! Having served on several interview committees, I know that numerous applications never reach the committee. They are thrown out and never given a second glance by the person who does the initial screening because they contain incomplete answers, misspellings or grammatical errors, including punctuation and sentence structure, writing in the margins, crossing or whiting out of words, and other types of errors.

As with the oral interview, you must assume that every question and/or item on the application has a purpose. Be sure that you take the time to read each section carefully; this presents you as a careful and accurate person. In the second sample application that follows, I have been told that many applicants misread the fourth page of *Application Sample 2* and circle number 6; these people have not followed the directions and show a lack of concern for accuracy.

The first sample application seems to be fairly standard for most districts and is easily filled out by most people. The second sample application is considered to be a more "grueling" application than many. If you can complete this application with confidence, you are most likely well prepared. I am including the entire application with the exception of the legal requirements, for example, drug policy, convictions, medical statements, and finger printing.

APPLICATION SAMPLE 1

ALL APPLICATIONS MUST BE TYPED. PLEASE ATTACH A COPY OF YOUR CREDENTIAL WITH THIS APPLICATION.

APPLICATION FOR POSITION REQUIRING CERTIFICATION

SS No._____   Date_____

Name_____
   (Last)   (First)   (Middle)   (Any other last name)

Home Phone_____Business Phone_____

Applying for: Regular Contract_____   Daily Substituting_____

Are you presently under contract?_____ Date you will be available_____

Current Employer_____

Immediate Supervisor_____
_____
_____

Name of Credential   **Subjects on Credential**   **Expiration Date**
_____
_____

Specific Credentialed Teaching   (1) _____ (3) _____
Expertise in Order of Preference: (2) _____ (4) _____
Number of Semester Hours earned after BA/BS_____
_____
_____

COLLEGE and/or UNIVERSITY TRAINING

Name of Institution - State - Major - Sem. Hours - Minor - Hours - Degree

_____

_____

_____

College distinctions, awards, or scholarships _____

_____

_____

_____

STUDENT TEACHING EXPERIENCE

<u>No. of Mos.</u> <u>School District</u> <u>School</u> <u>Supervising Teacher</u> <u>Assignment</u>

_____

_____

_____

_____

TEACHER ASSISTANT EXPERIENCE

<u>From</u> <u>To</u> <u>School District</u> <u>School</u> <u>Supervisor</u> <u>Assignment</u> <u>Grade Levels</u>

_____

_____

_____

_____

SUBSTITUTE TEACHING EXPERIENCE

From To School District Address City/State School Assignment Grades

_____

_____

_____

REGULAR CONTRACT TEACHING

From To School District Address City/State School Assignment Grades

_____

_____

_____

MILITARY EXPERIENCE

Branch of Service_____ Grade or Rank_____

_____

_____

WORK EXPERIENCE - Other than Teaching or Military including relevant volunteer or nonpaid experience

From	To	Employer	City/State	Type of Work

Any relevant volunteer or nonpaid experience? Please list:

_____

_____

_____

Where may we obtain your
PLACEMENT FILE?_____
Please give the name under
which your placement file
was originated_____File No._____

_____

_____

List the names of three people who are best qualified to know of your work professionally: (Administrators, Department Heads, College Professors, Supervising Teachers)

Name	Complete Mailing Address	Telephone	Position

Would you be interested in sponsoring the following? (Circle) 1. Drama 2. Key Club 3. Annual 4. School Paper 5. Speech/Debate 6. Drill Team 7. Athletic Club 8. A. S. B. 9. Booster Club !0. Other (List)
_____

Would you be interested in coaching? (list coaching assignments preferred) _____
_____

Have you ever been convicted of a crime?_____ If yes, describe in full (attach a sheet if necessary) _____

_____

_____
_____

Person to be notified in case of accident or emergency:

_____
    Name   Complete Address   Telephone

Additional comments (Please feel free to document special awards, personal involvement or other endeavors considered by you as significant when you are being considered as a candidate.)

_____

_____

_____
_____

I hereby certify that the statements above are true and complete to the best of my knowledge.

                       _____
                             Signature   Date

APPLICATION SAMPLE 2

This application must be completed by all certificated applicants to be considered for employment. It must be handwritten.

APPLICATION FOR CERTIFICATED PERSONNEL

Name_____Date_____

Position sought_____

List books you have read in the past five years which deal with new trends, concepts or findings in the field of teaching and learning. Indicate your impression of the book and its theory, etc.

TITLE	AUTHOR	THEORY

1. _____

2. _____

3. _____

4. _____
   _____

List and describe any new instructional or curriculum practices that you have learned and introduced into your teaching within the past two years.

TECHNIQUE	DESCRIPTION
1.	
2.	
3.	
4.	

List the names and locations of any schools you have visited and observed during the past two or three years where you learned something new that you now use in the classroom.

SCHOOL	PRACTICE
1.	
2.	
3.	
4.	

Describe at least one innovative technique that you taught to a colleague during the past two years.

_____

_____

_____

_____

_____

Explain how you successfully modified or adopted a new technique you have read about, heard about, or have seen in the past two or three years.

_____

_____

_____

_____

_____

On a scale of one to six (one being the highest) estimate your own ability to grow and to increase your professional skills and knowledge.

    Circle one: 1   2   3   4   5   6

    List specific evidence and support your rating of yourself.

_____

_____

_____

_____

_____

In a paragraph or two explain individualized instruction. How does it differ from a traditional program?

What is your concept of an open classroom?

Write a short description of the ability level, learning style, interest, talents, study habits, etc., of a typical student in the grade or specialty in which you are interested in teaching.

Write your understanding of the technique/learning process and include the various levels of learning.

PREPARING FOR THE INTERVIEW

The following questions are important because they deal with verbal and nonverbal messages. Think these questions through and be conscious of them during the interview.

Will you be certain of directions so that you arrive a few minutes early for the interview?

How do you greet the interviewer(s)? (By name, if possible, and offer your hand only if the interviewer does so first.)

Have you researched the school district, the school population, district or school programs, and the specific position for which you are applying? If at all possible, visit the area. Talk to people---get background information about the area.

Know why you want the position.

Be prepared philosophically on major education issues. Do your homework!

Do you have a strong handshake?

Are you dressed conservatively?

Do you smile? Do you demonstrate a sense of humor?

PREPARING FOR THE INTERVIEW

Do you appear comfortable?

Do you put others at ease?

Do you speak to everyone or just to one person?

Do you respond <u>positively</u>? (NEVER criticize a previous employer)

Are you energetic? Do you show vim and vigor?

As in the written application, do you assume that every question has a purpose?

Are your answers well organized?

Strive for brevity and clarity.

If it is a long question, do you summarize?

Do you appear to be conceited or a "know-it-all"?

Do you listen?

Do you demonstrate a willingness to learn?

Do you appear to be someone who will go the "extra mile"?

Do you look the interviewers in the eyes throughout the interview?

Are you tactful?

Can you take criticism?

Do you show enthusiasm?

Do you have a positive attitude?

Are you flexible?

Do you display intolerant or prejudicial attitudes?

Do you have varied interests?

Do you appear to be a person who genuinely cares about children?

Can you work within a team **and** alone?

Do you appear to be a happy, self-confident, and secure person?

Be who you are! A phony interview may get you a position you do not want and with which you can not work. Stick to your basic position and beliefs.

DO NOT carry materials into the interview with you (briefcase, reading material, notebook, etc.). Taking an example of a project you have taught would be an exception to this rule.

You may be asked to teach a sample lesson in front of the interview committee. View this as an opportunity to present yourself at your very best! This request should tell you that the district is concerned with quality and that they are truly seeking to hire the top candidate.

Thank the interview team and hope for the best!

THE INTERVIEW

In addition to the interview questions on the following pages, you must be clear in your thinking concerning these subjects:

Philosophy --- Know your personal philosophy of education. Be prepared to discuss and support your ideas.

State Framework --- It is important to have a copy of the State Framework. Know what the state requires, what the terminology means, and the current trends. This is true for all levels but especially for the secondary teacher who may be teaching in one or two subject areas.

Learning Styles --- Be ready to describe them and give practical suggestions as to how you would put them to use in the classroom.

ESL Students --- Have definite ideas of how you would plan for students in your class who speak English as a second language.

Special Education Students --- There are students who attend special education classes for certain subjects only and may be mainstreamed into your class. Develop a lesson plan of how you might teach these students and what resources you would use for support.

Discipline --- The current trend is "assertive discipline"; be able to expand on this trend.

REMEMBER that an interview is a two-way street. Not only are the interviewers taking a look at you, but you are seeking information about the district, the school, and the people with whom you would be working. Ask yourself, "Is this a place I really want to work?" <u>Believe in yourself, in your abilities, and in what you are offering the district</u>!

QUESTIONS

The questions on the following pages are not necessarily in any order of importance or organized in any specific manner other than level or particular teaching field. Essential questions are repeated in each area and/or teaching level. Questions that are unique to a specific teaching field and/or level are found in that section.

It is highly doubtful that any interview would include all of the questions in any section, but if you are prepared for the variety of questions presented here, you are well on your way to a successful interview. Good luck!

INTERVIEW QUESTIONS
Early Admittance to Kindergarten

1. What do you know about this district and the position for which you are applying?

2. What are the essential qualities of a good teacher?

3. Tell us about yourself. What is your greatest attribute? What area do you most need to strengthen?

4. What made you decide to become a teacher?

5. Describe your work experience during college or subsequent to college. What responsibilities did you have?

6. Explain your philosophy of an EAK program.

7. How would you set up your ideal classroom environment?

<u>Interviewer listen for</u>: Materials at children's eye level, walls/bulletin boards should be made by the children, housekeeping area, block area, art area, easels, circle area,

quiet reading area, etc.; the room should be centered around the children and their needs.

8. What does "multimedia" mean to you?

9. How can multimedia be used to enhance learning?

10. How can multimedia be used to vary instruction?

11. Given unlimited funding, how would you instruct students using multimedia?

12. How would you go about setting up a year-long program?

13. What experiences have you had with four and five year olds?

14. Describe your work experience during college or subsequent to college. What responsibilities did you have?

15. Explain your philosophy of an EAK program.

16. Describe the difference between pre-school EAK.

17. Describe the difference between EAK and Kindergarten.

18. What do you see as the role of the parent, and how would you directly involve them in your program?

INTERVIEW QUESTIONS - EAK

19. How would you prepare students/families for the transition into Kindergarten?

20. How would you teach essential concepts to children. i.e., social/emotional?

<u>Interviewer listen for</u>: Housekeeping, games, puppets, stories, circle time, etc.

21. Describe specific activities for the following areas and give examples of how they could be integrated:

> Reading Readiness
> Math Readiness
> Physical Education
> Art
> Music

22. What involvement, if any, should regular Kindergarten teachers have in an EAK program?

23. What is your philosophy on approaches to discipline?

24. How would you use volunteers?

25. If there are two classes with 25 students each and a 40 minute overlap, what type of activities would you plan during the 40 minutes?

INTERVIEW QUESTIONS - EAK

26. In your field which areas are particular strengths, and which areas need development? How do you work toward improving these areas? Tell us of other specialties you have.

<u>Interviewer listen for</u>: Self-confidence, honesty, seeking support from others in area of weakness and/or <u>a willingness to learn new skills</u>.

27. I noticed in your application that you listed _____ by _____ as a book you recently read. Tell me how you feel about his/her views on _____.

28. Our state appears to be headed toward year-round schools. How do you feel about teaching year-round?

29. If you are selected for this position, what can we expect from you, and what qualities would you bring that would enhance the educational program in _____ School District and at _____ School?

30. Is there anything else you would like to tell us about yourself that would help us in making our decision?

INTERVIEW QUESTIONS - EAK

INTERVIEWER'S SUBJECTIVE RATINGS:

1. Confidence, poise, warmth, humor (1 to 10 points) _____

2. Is this teaching candidate someone you would like to work with and/or someone you would like to have as a teacher for your own child? (1 to 10 points) _____

INTERVIEW QUESTIONS
Elementary Level

1. What do you know about this district and the position for which you are applying?

2. Tell us about yourself. What is your greatest attribute? What area do you most need to strengthen?

3. Describe your work experience during college or subsequent to college. What responsibilities did you have?

4. What made you decide to become a teacher?

5. How would you go about setting up a new classroom and establishing a year-long plan?

6. What is the relationship of lesson planning, objectives, and goals to a successful curriculum?

7. How would you determine the placement of a new child in your curriculum?

INTERVIEW QUESTIONS - ELEMENTARY

8. We place a lot of emphasis on writing in this district. Can you tell us of one actual lesson you have used to develop your students' writing abilities?

9. How often would you have students write?

10. Regarding your writing activity, give us some examples of the kind of structure you would provide for fourth graders.

11. How does spelling, punctuation, and basic grammar tie in with the creative writing process?

12. What does "multimedia" mean to you?

13. What specific experience have you had with multimedia such as VCR's, CD ROM, laser disc players, video camcorders, etc.?

14. How can multimedia be used to enhance learning?

15. How can multimedia be used to vary instruction?

16. How can multimedia be used to present varied individual and whole-group instruction?

17. What types of multimedia are virtually all students exposed to in their homes on a daily basis?

18. Given unlimited funding, how would you instruct students using multimedia?

19. Do you feel comfortable teaching physical education?

20. If you are teaching adapted physical education, how would you consult with the special education teacher regarding the needs of your students?

21. In your field which areas are particular strengths, and which areas need development? How do you work toward improving these areas? Tell us of other specialties you have.

<u>Interviewer listen for</u>: Self-confidence, honesty, seeking support from others in areas of weakness and/or <u>a willingness to learn new skills.</u>

22. What are the essential qualities of a good teacher?

23. Are you familiar with Clinical Teaching? If so, please describe the process. (If you are not familiar with Clinical Teaching, see "Suggested Reading List", page 94).

<u>Interviewer listen for</u>: Clinical Teaching process, set, motivation, input, modeling, etc.

INTERVIEW QUESTIONS - ELEMENTARY

24. After giving a state-mandated test and receiving results for each student in each subject area tested, what would you do with these results?

25. How would you motivate your students to want to learn_____?

26. How important is collaborative learning in the classroom? Are there some models you can discuss with us?

27. Describe your procedures for managing student discipline and for fostering positive human relationships within your classroom.

<u>Interviewer listen for</u>: Systematic procedures such as having clearly revealed expectations; following through with consequences if warnings are given; having students contract for and commit to future positive behaviors; dealing with students individually; developing an atmosphere of mutual respect; inclusion of parents.

28. In terms of student achievement what would you expect your class to accomplish in one year? How would you grade a student who works hard but performs below grade level?

29. Outside of academics, what would you expect your students to have gained after having had you as a teacher?

INTERVIEW QUESTIONS - ELEMENTARY

30. What involvement should parents have in the schools?

31. Describe your philosophy regarding homework.

32. What grade level would you prefer to teach? What are your first, second, and third choices?

33. Tell us about your philosophy of reading and describe the type of reading program you would establish for a first grade class.

34. A student is having trouble learning the alphabet. How would you help the student?

35. Are you familiar with the new math and language arts framework? Please tell us about them?

36. How would you introduce the concept of addition?

37. We are looking for someone to help us with a music program. How would you go about setting up a new music program and establishing a year-long plan?

38. For what kinds of music programs have you been responsible? Involved?

39. How would you involve parents in establishing a music program?

Interviewer listen for: Leadership skills, the ability to delegate responsibility, and creative ideas for using parental assistance.

40. How could you assist a classroom teacher, and what types of activities would you plan?

Interviewer listen for: creativity, integration of music into the curriculum, working within a team.

41. What is an effective staff member? What characteristics do you have that would fit you into this description?

42. If you were teaching a unit on mammals in second grade, how would you integrate other curriculum areas?

43. Please share the system of communication with parents that you plan to implement in your classroom.

44. A student is having trouble learning multiplication tables. How would you help the student?

Interviewer listen for: Tries to discover why or in what way the student is having the problem OR searches for a way that would work best for this individual student.

45. If you were teaching a unit on the ocean, how would you integrate other curriculum areas?

46. If a grade level made a decision concerning the math curriculum and you disagreed, how would you handle the situation?

47. In your opinion is it necessary for the student to like the teacher in order for the student to learn?

48. I noticed in your application that you listed _____ by _____ as a book you recently read. Tell me how you feel about his/her views on _____.

49. Describe what a continuum means to you and how it can be used.

50. You find yourself in a conference with a very hostile parent. This conference is occurring after numerous attempts to get the parent to come in for a conference. The child is doing poorly, assignments are incomplete, and behavior is unacceptable. How will you present this information to the parent?

51. How would you respond to a parent who strongly presented you with the following information:

    A. "I feel that you are not sending home enough homework."

INTERVIEW QUESTIONS - ELEMENTARY

    B. "The homework you do send home is unimportant."

    C. "I feel that you are picking on my child."

52. Tell us your perception and expectation of communication in the school between:
    - A. Teacher and Principal
    - B. Teacher and Parent
    - C. Teacher and Student
    - D. Teacher and Teacher
    - E. Teacher and Classified Personnel

53. What standards of behavior would you expect from the students during a _____ lesson?

54. How would you teach _____ to a class of students with varying abilities?

55. The reform movement in restructuring schools explicitly discusses authentic assessment of students with portfolios. Can you tell us how you would use a portfolio toward this end?

56. What kinds of activities can schools provide that will promote the bonding of students to their school?

57. Our state appears to be heading toward year-round schools. How do you feel about teaching year-round?

INTERVIEW QUESTIONS - ELEMENTARY

58. If you are selected for this position, what can we expect from you, and what qualities would you bring that would enhance the educational program in _____Elementary School and _____School District?

<u>Interviewer listen for</u>: Positive attitude, flexibility, enthusiasm, team player, cooperation, open mind.

59. Is there anything else you would like to tell us about yourself that would help us in making our decision?

INTERVIEWER'S SUBJECTIVE RATINGS:

1. Confidence, poise, warmth, humor (1 to 10 points) _____

2. Is this teaching candidate someone you would like to work with and/or someone you would like to have as a teacher for your child? (1 to 10 points) _____

INTERVIEW QUESTIONS
Middle School Level

1. What do you know about this district and the position for which you are applying?

2. Tell us about yourself. What is your greatest attribute? What area do you most need to strengthen?

3. Describe your work experience during college or subsequent to college. What responsibilities did you have?

4. What made you decide to become a teacher?

5. What is important in setting up a new classroom and establishing a year-long plan?

6. What is the relationship of lesson planning, objectives, and goals to a successful curriculum?

7. In your field which areas are particular strengths, and which areas need development? How do you work toward improving these areas? Tell us of other specialties you have.

<u>Interviewer listen for</u>: Self-confidence, honesty, seeking others for support in weak areas and/or <u>a willingness to learn new skills</u>.

8. Describe your procedures for managing student discipline and for fostering positive human relationships within your classroom.

<u>Interviewer listen for</u>: Systematic procedures such as having clearly revealed expectations; following through with consequences if warnings are given; having students contract for and commit to future positive behavior; dealing with students individually; developing an atmosphere of mutual respect; inclusion of parents.

9. Tell us your philosophy of middle schools. Do you favor a core program or departmentalization?

10. We are committed to the Middle School "family" for our students. How do you feel about sharing a smaller number of students and planning closely with another teacher?

11. Can you give examples of how social studies and language arts or math and science can be integrated?

12. How important is collaborative learning in the classroom? Are there some models you can discuss with us?

13. What are some methods middle school teachers can utilize to ensure that limited-English-proficient students have access to the critical thinking curriculum?

14. Describe today's middle school student developmentally.

15. What does "multimedia" mean to you?

16. What specific experience have you had with multimedia such as VCR's, CD ROM, laser disc players, video camcorders, etc.?

17. How can multimedia be used to enhance learning?

18. How can multimedia be used to vary instruction?

19. How can multimedia be used to present varied individual and whole-group instruction?

20. What types of multimedia are virtually all students exposed to in their homes on a daily basis?

21. Given unlimited funding, how would you instruct students using multimedia?

22. We believe that every middle school student needs to develop learning strategies that are directed toward the goal of

becoming an independent learner. Would you be willing to teach a study skills class with this direction and goal?

23. Can you discuss the value of an exploratory/enrichment wheel?

24. The reform movement in restructuring schools explicitly discusses authentic assessment of students with portfolios. Can you tell us how you would use a portfolio toward this end?

25. If your grade level team made a decision about discipline procedures and you didn't agree, how would you handle the situation?

26. Are you familiar with Clinical Teaching? If so please describe the procedure. (If you are not familiar with Clinical Teaching, see "Suggested Reading List").

<u>Interviewer listen for</u>: Clinical Teaching process set, motivation, input, modeling, etc.

27. If you were teaching a unit on the American Revolution, how would you integrate other curricular areas?

28. We place a lot of emphasis on writing in this district. Can you tell us of one actual lesson you have used to develop your students' writing abilities?

INTERVIEW QUESTIONS - MIDDLE SCHOOL

29. How often would you have students write?

30. What are the essential qualities of a good teacher?

31. How would you teach _____ to a class of students with varying abilities?

32. How would you grade a student who works hard but performs below grade level?

33. Outside of academics what would you expect your students to have gained after having had you as a teacher?

34. Describe your philosophy concerning homework?

35. What involvement should parents have in the schools?

36. Describe what a continuum means to you and how it can be used.

37. How would you respond to a parent who strongly presented you with the following information:
    A. "I feel that you are not sending home enough homework."
    B. "The homework you do sent home is unimportant."
    C. "I think there is a personality clash between you and my child. I feel that you are picking on him."

38. We are looking for someone to help us with a music program. How would you go about setting up a new music program and establishing a year-long plan?

39. For what kinds of music programs have you been responsible? Involved?

40. How would you involve parents in establishing a music program?

<u>Interviewer listen for</u>: Leadership skills, the ability to delegate responsibility, and creative ideas for using parental assistance.

41. How could you assist a classroom teacher, and what types of activities would you plan?

<u>Interviewer listen for</u>: Creativity, integration of music into the curriculum, working within a team.

42. In your opinion is it necessary for a student to like a teacher in order for the student to learn?

43. We believe teachers should be coaches, and students should be collaborative, active learners. Can you tell us of a unit in which you participated that aligns itself with this statement?

INTERVIEW QUESTIONS - MIDDLE SCHOOL

44. For what extracurricular activity would you be willing to be responsible?

45. You are teaching an adapted physical education class. How would you consult with the special eduction teacher regarding the needs of your students?

46. What are your perceptions and expectations of communication in the school between:

    A. Teacher and Principal
    B. Teacher and Parent
    C. Teacher and Student
    D. Teacher and Teacher
    E. Teacher and Classified Personnel

47. What qualities do you have that would enable you to be an effective teacher of adolescents?

<u>Interviewer listen for</u>: Knowledge of adolescents, flexibility, compassion, understanding but firm.

48. I noticed in your application that you listed _____ by _____ as a book you recently read. Tell me what you think about his/her views on _____.

49. It appears that our state is moving toward year-round schools. How do you feel about teaching in a year-round school?

50. What kinds of activities can schools provide that will promote the bonding of students to their school?

51. If you are selected for this position, what can we expect from you and what qualities would you bring that would enhance the educational program in _____District and at _____Middle School?

<u>Interviewer listen for</u>: Positive attitude, flexibility, enthusiasm, cooperation, team player, open mind.

52. Is there anything else you would like to tell us about yourself that would help us in making our decision?

INTERVIEWER'S SUBJECTIVE RATINGS:

1. Confidence, poise, warmth, humor (1 to 10 points) _____

2. Is this teaching candidate someone you would like to work with and/or someone you would like to have as a teacher for your child? (1 to 10 points)

INTERVIEW QUESTIONS - MIDDLE SCHOOL

SPECIFIC QUESTIONS IN SUBJECT AREAS

Every teaching candidate should purchase through your college/university book store the State Framework for your grade level and/or your specific teaching areas. Know the framework well, be familiar with the terminology, and be prepared with specific examples of how you have worked and will work within the framework.

INTERVIEW QUESTIONS
High School Level

Interview questions at the high school level tend to be directed less in the specific content area and more in the areas of philosophy, school policies, being a part of an academic department, classroom management, and teaching techniques. The questions listed on the following pages could be ask in an interview by a panel in any academic department. More specific questions for various subjects follow.

1. What do you know about this district and the position for which you are applying?

2. What do you know about our high school?

3. Tell us something about your background, training, and work experience.

4. Describe today's high school student.

5. Why did you choose teaching as a career?

INTERVIEW QUESTIONS - HIGH SCHOOL

6. Describe your classroom management procedures.

7. Tell us your philosophy of teaching students with lower ability.

8. What special skills do you think are necessary for teaching remedial students? Give an example of one such skill as applied to a class of students who have not experienced much success academically.

9. Define the "Art of Teaching".

10. What does "multimedia" mean to you?

11. What specific experience have you had with multimedia such as VCR's, CD ROM, laser disc players, video camcorders, etc.?

12. How can multimedia be used to enhance learning?

13. How can multimedia be used to vary instruction?

14. How can multimedia be used to present varied individual and whole-group instruction?

15. What types of multimedia are virtually all students exposed to in their homes on a daily basis?

16. Given unlimited funding, how would you instruct students using multimedia?

17. How would you meet the needs of the higher achievers while limiting the course content to meet the needs of the lower achiever in a heterogeneous classroom?

18. How important is collaborative learning in the classroom? Are there some models you can discuss with us?

19. We believe that teachers should be coaches, and students should be collaborative, active learners. Can you tell us of a unit or project in which you participated that aligns itself with this statement?

20. The reform movement in restructuring schools explicitly discusses authentic assessment of students with portfolios. Can you tell us how you would use a portfolio toward this end?

21. If you were in a tracked program, what level would you prefer? How would you adjust to teaching a level you did not particularly desire?

22. On any given day, if we walked into your classroom, what would you typically be doing? What kinds of activities would the students typically be doing?

INTERVIEW QUESTIONS - HIGH SCHOOL

23. What behavioral standards do you intend to establish for your classroom?

24. Our high school is strict regarding school and district policies. How would you handle tardiness, absences, and disciplinary referrals?

25. When do you think it is appropriate to call parents?

26. In what order of importance would you rank the following:

   A. Teaching style
   B. Knowledge of subject matter
   C. Rapport with students

27. If you discover that at the end of a grading period you have given more "D's" and "F's" than other teachers in your department or the district average, what, if anything, would you do about the situation?

28. In your opinion what are some of the reasons students do not learn?

29. Explain your philosophy concerning homework. What is the purpose of the homework assigned by you?

30. How many preparations per day can a teacher handle successfully?

31. How do you evaluate students? What kind of grading system do you use?

32. What type of organizational system would you use to keep students apprised of their current grades?

33. How would you feel about team teaching?

34. Describe a lesson in which you used cooperative learning as one of your teaching strategies.

35. How would you plan and teach an integrated thematic unit?

36. On a scale of one to ten, how would you rate yourself as a teacher?

37. What kinds of activities can schools provide that will promote the bonding of students to their school?

38. What would be your role in helping us to achieve and maintain a cohesive, efficient, and dedicated _____ Department?

INTERVIEW QUESTIONS - HIGH SCHOOL

39. In your field which areas are particular strengths, and which areas need development? How do you work toward improving these areas? Tell us of other specialties you have.

40. What are your personal goals and objectives? What do you expect and want to be doing five years from now?

41. How do you think your most recent employer would describe you?

42. How do you think your friends would describe you?

43. Our state appears to be heading toward year-round schools. How do you feel about teaching year-round?

44. If you are selected for this position, what can we expect from you and what qualities would you bring that would enhance the educational program in _____ School District and at _____ High School?

45. Do you have any questions you would like to ask us?

46. Is there anything you would like to tell us about yourself that would help us in making our decision?

INTERVIEW QUESTIONS - HIGH SCHOOL

INTERVIEWER'S SUBJECTIVE RATINGS:

1. Confidence, poise, warmth, humor (1 to 10 points) _____

2. Is this teaching candidate someone you would like to work with and/or someone you would like to have as a teacher for your own child? (1 to 10 points) _____

High School Level Questions in Academic Areas

Science

1. Pick three subjects within the field of science (chemistry, physics, biology, etc.). Which would be the easiest, which would be a moderate challenge, and which would be the most difficult for you to teach?

2. Choose a topic within the field you think would be a moderate challenge for you and give us a brief overview of how you would teach this unit.

3. The Science State Framework suggests that forty percent of a unit should be activity based. Why are activity-based lessons better than a standard textbook approach?

4. What types of things would you do to work within this framework?

5. What kinds of investigations would you have in your science classes?

6. Can you give examples of how science and math can be integrated?

Mathematics

1. How would you use manipulatives in the classroom? How would you get the students involved in using manipulatives?

2. Do you ever use small-group instruction or cooperative learning groups?

3. How would you use "writing across the curriculum" in your program?

4. Would you have students describe in writing the process of solving a problem?

5. What kinds of "real life" problems do you use?

6. Give examples of short, medium, and long-term projects you might assign.

7. How do you get students to think through problem solving instead of simply doing the memorized steps?

8. What kinds of investigations would you have in your math classes?

9. Can give examples of how math and science can be integrated?

Language Arts

1. How does grammar relate to the successful teaching of writing?

2. What is your experience with the CAP (California Assessment Program) writing assignments? (Out-of-state teachers using this book will substitute the method of assessment used in your state)

3. Choose any piece of literature that would be found in a high school Language Arts class and suggest what you think would be a good question for a thirty-minute writing test.

4. How do you feel about team teaching?

5. How do you feel about teaching a core class of Language Arts and Social Science?

6. Can you give examples of how language arts and social science can be integrated?

64 HIGH SCHOOL QUESTIONS - ACADEMIC AREAS

Social Science

1. U.S. History now covers only the 20th century because of the new California State Model Curriculum Standards. The extra four months that you now have available to you for this course is "extra time". How will you use this time to enhance your students' learning?

2. What is your experience with the CAP (California Assessment Program) testing in the social sciences? (Out-of-state teachers using this booklet will substitute the method of assessment used in your state)

3. How would you use "writing across the curriculum" in your program?

4. How do you feel about team teaching?

5. How do you feel about teaching a core class of social science and language arts?

6. Can you give examples of how social science and language arts can be integrated?

HIGH SCHOOL QUESTIONS - ACADEMIC AREAS

Home Economics

1. In which areas of Home Economics do you consider yourself to be particularly strong?

2. If you did not have a curriculum guide, how would you plan a Child Development Program?

3. Procedurally, how would you set up the Child Development Program?

4. How would you handle parents who wish to discuss the sex education part of child development with you?

5. We feel that the clothing program needs some new ideas. What might you be able to bring to this program?

6. What role would academics play in the clothing classroom?

7. How would you use "writing across the curriculum" in your program?

8. Tell us about the FHA-HERO programs in a high school and how they fit into the home economics program.

9. We want to increase enrollment in our home economics classes. What might you do to increase interest in the home economics program?

Physical Education

It is essential that you visit the school site before you interview for a teaching position in physical education. Talk to a present employee and ask to have a tour of the facilities. You will want to know what is available to you: How large is the gym? How many tennis courts? How many handball courts? What equipment is available and in good working order? What are the present strengths and weakness of the physical education program? In other words, anticipate questions that might arise and be prepared with strategies and suggestions.

1. We need help with school morale, the intramural program, the integrity of the physical education program, etc. Can you give us a rough idea of what might be of help to us in this area?

2. Do you have a particular area of expertise?

3. Do you teach life skills?

4. Safety is a primary concern for us. How do you teach and maintain safety, control, and student interest?

5. You have sixty to eighty students by yourself. How do you manage them?

6. How would you run a tennis class with sixty students and eight courts?

7. You have a situation where a student is not following instructions. What strategy would you use to get him/her to cooperate?

8. What do you do if someone becomes injured?

9. Are you willing to participate in extra-curricular activities such as being the advisor to the Lettermen's Club?

10. Have you ever taught an interdisciplinary unit --- one that might involve physical education, mathematics, biology, language arts, etc.?

11. These are the facilities we have. How are you going to use the facilities?

INTERVIEW QUESTIONS
Special Day Class

1. What do you know about this district and the position for which you are applying?

2. What made you decide to become a teacher?

3. As a Special Day Class teacher you will have students in your class with a wide range of abilities and behaviors. Describe how you would set up a program to meet a wide range of needs.

4. Tell us about yourself. What is your greatest attribute? What area do you most need to strengthen?

5. Describe your classroom management system.

6. How would you determine the placement of a new child in your curriculum?

7. Describe your work experience during college or subsequent to college. What responsibilities did you have?

INTERVIEW QUESTIONS - SPECIAL DAY CLASS

8. Describe your procedure for managing student discipline and for fostering positive human relationships within your classroom.

<u>Interviewer listen for</u>: Systematic procedures such as having clearly revealed expectations; following through with consequences if warnings are given; having students contract for and commit to future positive behaviors; dealing with students individually; developing an atmosphere of mutual respect; inclusion of parents.

9. How would you communicate and articulate your program with the regular education program? How would you assist the regular classroom teacher?

10. What are the essential qualities of a good teacher?

11. What do you see as the role of a Resource Specialist?

12. What does "multimedia" mean to you?

13. What specific experience have you had with multimedia such as VCR's, CD ROM, laser disc players, video camcorders, etc.?

14. How can multimedia be used to enhance learning?

15. How can multimedia be used to vary instruction?

16. How can multimedia be used to present varied individual and whole-group instruction?

17. What types of multimedia are virtually all students exposed to in their homes on a daily basis?

18. Given unlimited funding, how would you instruct students using multimedia?

19. From the initial teacher contact regarding a student having problems, what are the steps you would follow?

20. What are some techniques you might use to measure changed student behavior?

21. What kinds of clues might you obtain by observing the student's behavior during the assessment process?

22. How does the assessment process relate to instructional objectives and instructional procedures?

23. Describe your philosophy regarding homework.

24. Describe what a continuum means to you and how it can be used.

INTERVIEW QUESTIONS - SPECIAL DAY CLASS

25. In your field which areas are particular strengths, and which areas need development? How do you work toward improving these areas? Tell us of other specialties you have.

<u>Interviewer listen for</u>: Self-confidence, honesty, seeking support from others in areas of weakness, and/or a willingness to learn new skills.

26. What do you consider to be your most successful teaching experience? Describe the instructional strategies/techniques used.

27. How would you respond to a parent who strongly presented you with the following information:

    A. "I feel that the work you are having my child do is inconsequential."
    B. "I want my child put back in regular classes where he will do real work."
    C. "I feel that you are picking on my child."

28. You find yourself in a conference with a very hostile parent. This conference is occurring after numerous attempts to get the parent to come in for a conference. The child is doing poorly---assignments are incomplete and behavior is unacceptable. How will you present this information to the parent?

INTERVIEW QUESTIONS - SPECIAL DAY CLASS

29. What involvement should parents have in the school?

30. What grade level would you prefer to teach? What are your first, second, and third choices?

31. How do you measure student/program effectiveness?

32. Outside of academics what would you expect your students to have gained after having had you as a teacher?

33. In your opinion is it necessary for the student to like the teacher in order for the student to learn?

34. I noticed in your application that you listed_____ by_____ as a book you recently read. Tell me how you feel about his/her views on _____.

35. Tell us your perceptions and expectations of communication in the school between:

    A. Teacher and Principal
    B. Teacher and Parent
    C. Teacher and Student
    D. Teacher and Teacher
    E. Teacher and Classified Personnel

INTERVIEW QUESTIONS - SPECIAL DAY CLASS

36. What is your experience in writing IEP goals and objectives? Give examples of typical goals and objectives.

37. What do you consider to be your most successful teaching experience? Describe the instructional strategies/techniques used.

38. Our state appears to be moving toward year-round schools. How do you feel about teaching year-round?

39. If you are selected for this position, what can we expect from you, and what qualities would you bring that would enhance the Special Education program in the _____School District and at _____ School?

40. Is there anything else you would like to tell us about yourself that would help us in making our decision?

INTERVIEWER'S SUBJECTIVE RATING:

1. Confidence, poise, warmth, humor (1 to 10 points) _____

2. Is this teaching candidate someone you would like to work with and/or someone you would like to have as a teacher for your own child? (1 to 10 points) _____

INTERVIEW QUESTIONS
Bilingual Teacher

1. What do you know about this district and the position for which you are applying?

2. What made you decide to become a teacher?

3. Describe your work experiences during college or subsequent to college. What responsibilities did you have?

4. What instructional materials for bilingual classrooms are you familiar with and which do you prefer?

5. How are Limited English Proficient students identified?

6. How does the organization of a bilingual classroom differ from the "regular" classroom?

7. What does "multimedia" mean to you?

INTERVIEW QUESTIONS - BILINGUAL CLASS

8. What specific experience have you had with multimedia such as VCR's, CD ROM, laser disc players, video camcorders, etc.?

9. How can multimedia be used to enhance learning?

10. How can multimedia be used to vary instruction?

11. How can multimedia be used to present varied individual and whole-group instruction?

12. What types of multimedia are virtually all students exposed to in their homes on a daily basis?

13. Given unlimited funding, how would you instruct students using multimedia?

14. What are some important differences between a transitional bilingual program and a maintenance bilingual program?

15. What are the essential qualities of a good teacher?

16. A parent is unsure about placing a child in your bilingual classroom. What would you tell the parent to assure him/her that this placement is the most advantageous for the child?

INTERVIEW QUESTIONS - BILINGUAL CLASS

17. You find yourself in a conference with a very hostile parent. The conference is occurring after numerous attempts to get the parent to come in for a conference. The child is doing poorly, does not follow your instructions, and the behavior is unacceptable. How would you present this information to the parent?

18. Do you think it is necessary for the student to like the teacher in order to learn?

19. How would you respond to a parent who presented you with the following information:

    A. "I do not feel that my child is making fast enough progress in English."
    B. "My child does not like to come to you for help with English. There must be something wrong with the way you are teaching."
    C. "I feel that you are picking on my child."

20. What involvement should parents have in the school?

21. In you bilingual classroom how would you teach language arts? Math? Reading?

22. Describe your philosophy regarding homework.

INTERVIEW QUESTIONS - BILINGUAL CLASS

23. Outside of academics what would you expect your students to have gained after having had you as a teacher?

24. Which grade level to you prefer to teach? What are your first, second, and third choices?

25. There are several recognized authors and researchers in the field of bilingual education. Which of them are you familiar with, and can you characterize their work?

26. In a staff meeting what would you tell your colleagues about the following three concerns: second language acquisition, sheltered English, and the natural approach?

27. In your field which areas are particular strengths, and which areas need development? How do you work toward improving these areas? Tell us of other specialties you have.

<u>Interviewer listen for</u>: Self-confidence, honesty, seeking support from others in areas of weakness and/or <u>a willingness to learn new skills</u>.

28. Tell us your perception and expectations of communication in the school between:

    A. Teacher and Principal
    B. Teacher and Parent
    C. Teacher and Student

INTERVIEW QUESTIONS - BILINGUAL CLASS

    D. Teacher and Teacher
    E. Teacher and Classified Personnel

29. Our state appears to be heading toward year-round schools. How do you feel about teaching year-round?

30. If you are selected for this position, what can we expect from you, and what qualities would you bring that would enhance the education program in _____ School District and at _____ School?

31. <u>Interviewer listen for</u>: Positive attitude, flexibility, enthusiasm, cooperation, team player, open mind.

32. Is there anything else you would like to tell us about yourself that would help us in making our decision?

INTERVIEWER'S SUBJECTIVE RATINGS:

1. Confidence, poise, warmth, humor (1 to 10 points) _____

2. Is this teaching candidate someone you would like to work with and/or someone you would like to have as a teacher for your own child? (1 to 10 points) _____

POST-INTERVIEW FOLLOW-UP TECHNIQUES

As quickly as possible after the interview, write down any questions for which you felt unprepared. Doing this is one more step toward gaining the confidence you want before the next interview.

You might wish to drop the interviewer a handwritten note thanking him/her for the time spent with you and expressing again your interest in the position. Mention something specific that was said or occurred during the interview. This is not only a gracious act, but taking the time to do this will bring your name to attention once again. Also, more likely than not, it will separate you from the other candidates.

If you are not chosen for the position, do not view it as rejection or failure on your part. It may be that you needed to be better prepared, or it may be that you gave the "perfect" interview. The person selected may have had more experience or may have been known in the district as a substitute or may have been selected for any other number of reasons. Do not be discouraged---view the interview as a stepping stone to getting the position you want. In fact, you should interview as often as someone will talk to you; the more often you go through the interview experience, the more adept you will become, and, thus, you will improve your chances each time.

POST-INTERVIEW FOLLOW-UP TECHNIQUES

It is also a good idea to call the principal (or whoever was in charge of the interview) in order to set up an appointment to discuss how you could have interviewed more successfully. Which answers needed improvement? What suggestions would the person make to you that would be of help in the future? You are seeking answers that may be very helpful, and most people will be happy to assist you. Not only can the information be invaluable, but you are also presenting yourself as a person who is willing to learn and as one who is flexible. Asking for this kind of help says to the employer that you are truly interested in a position in that particular district.

Be prepared! Trust and believe in yourself! If you persevere, you will eventually get the teaching position you want!

USING SUBSTITUTE TEACHING TO GET STARTED

Working as a substitute teacher has long been recognized as one path to getting a teaching position. If the school district is not currently hiring, or if you interviewed and were not selected for a teaching position, substitute teaching gives you an opportunity to present yourself as someone they would like to have as a permanent staff member. Substitute teaching also allows the teacher to realistically observe a particular school district, providing an opportunity both to meet principals, teachers, and students and to determine whether or not this is a place you want to teach.

Successful substitute teachers offer the following suggestions to the person who is striving for a teaching contract:

1. Know the school district geographically. You never want to be lost and not on time.

2. When arriving at a school site, know the name of the person for whom you are substituting. The person who

does the calling for substitute teachers will give you this information.

3. Remember the names of key personnel: principal, vice-principal, secretary, counselor, and other grade-level teachers.

4. Introduce yourself to the teachers who are teaching next door to your classroom. Be friendly, positive, and open to suggestions.

5. <u>Be fully prepared to improvise</u> if there are no lessons plans or if the lesson plans are inadequate.

6. If you have carefully read the "sub lesson plans" and do not fully understand them, stay calm and proceed to the best of your ability.

7. Classroom management is the proving ground of success or failure for many substitute teachers. It is of primary concern to administrators. If the administrator is put in a position of having to help a teacher control a class, he/she may ask, "If I have to do this person's job, why do I need him/her?"

8. Always be friendly, positive, and as helpful as possible to the district's substitute caller. Willingness to go the extra mile will often result in your being high on the list of

those substitute teachers called most often. This is what you want: an opportunity to prove who and what you are!

A SUPERINTENDENT'S PERSPECTIVE
An Interview with Dr. Jere Ancell
Alpine Union School District
Alpine, California

1. Question: In this district do you do the initial screening of teacher candidates? If so, why do you feel it is important?

Dr. Ancell: Yes. I see this initial screening process as a top priority. One of my major responsibilities is to ensure that we have top-quality candidates. And, yes, it does give me control. An institution is only as good as its personnel; if this idea is not adhered to closely, we will fail in producing a quality program. I also have a keen interest in it. If you can hire the good teacher candidates, everything else happens---the teacher is the key!

2. How important do you think it is to have a teacher candidate acquaint him/herself with the school and district prior to the interview?

Dr. Ancell: Very important. I think it really does a couple of things. First, it gives the candidate a sense of whether or not he or she would like to be a part of this district. Secondly, they know what the district is about; they've done their homework; it's in their favor. I like that. It shows sincere interest. It is really important that the person find out about operations, socio-economic student population, textbooks.

3. Question: How important are the cover letter, the resumé, and the application?

A SUPERINTENDENT'S PERSPECTIVE

Dr. Ancell: They are really important in that they send a message. If they are well done---neat, typed or handwritten (whatever is asked for on the forms)---it tells me that this person took the time, energy, and expense to do an excellent job. This position is important to them.

When I go through the paperwork, I can tell whether I want or don't want a person. The papers in front of me reflect the standards of the person. It's a reflection of the standards they would have for kids---a reflection of their teaching.

The message to get to candidates is, "Do your homework; be prepared; really study the application." How the paperwork is completed tells you if they are concerned.

4. Question: What are the most important characteristics of a teaching candidate?

Dr. Ancell: I believe the following are important: One, knowledge base; two, being familiar with the framework; three, teaching knowledge/learning theory; four, enthusiasm; five, being flexible; six, having a sense of humor; seven, being positive; eight, believing that kids are important.

5. Question: Do you think these characteristics are different at the elementary, middle school, and high school levels?

Dr. Ancell: No, I believe the characteristics of any good teacher are the same no matter what the level. It is just as important at the high school level to have the above traits as it is to have them at the elementary level.

6. Question: If a teacher candidate interviewed in this district and did not get the position, what would be your response if that person called for an appointment with you to discuss the interview and why he/she was not hired?

Dr. Ancell: I would welcome it. I've had that happen. They have asked, "What could I have done better?', "What was the deciding factor?" After having discussed the first interview, we have had situations where the person came back, interviewed for another position, and was successful. I think it says a lot.

I've called people back who weren't selected and told them where they were strong and why they didn't get the job. People always respond positively.

7. Question: Do you ever call former employers?

Dr. Ancell: Oh, yes! We always check references. It's a way of either confirming your opinion or of getting a different perspective. Sometimes you have to be really careful who you call---just who the person lists as a reference can tell you a lot.

8. Question: What are some suggestions you would offer a teacher candidate so that he/she might be more at ease during an interview?

Dr. Ancell: I think it helps if the person can become familiar with the setting of the inteview. Go to the district, know the location so that you are not hurried---this helps to create a comfort level. There is a fine line between talking too much and talking too little. Try to be natural. Don't take yourself too seriously---smile, laugh, show that you're a peson. So many times interviewers will say, "I really like that person." If you feel comfortable around someone, you will probably work well with that person.

9. Question: What unspoken clues do you consider that might indicate to you whether or not a teacher candidate

would be a good "match" with the community, a specific principal, a grade level, and/or subject area?

Dr. Ancell: Appearance, how the person presents him or herself. For example, do they look too relaxed, not relaxed enough, uptight? Do they try to impress the interviewers with vocabulary? Are there any unusual mannerisms? For example, fidgeting, chewing gum, little eye contact?

10. All things being equal, do you ever make a decision for one candidate over another on a "gut level" feeling?

Dr. Ancell: Yes, I do. There is just something about the person that says, "This person is it." And, then there is the person who has all the right answers, but there is something that just doesn't click.

One thing we try to do in this district that really helps us to decide is to have the candidates come back and teach a lesson to a classroom of kids. Some have great interviews but don't do well with the students. Some have had less than glowing interviews, but you think there might be something about this person that you are missing. When you watch them in the classroom, you see them interacting with students and say to yourself, "This is it. This person can do it."

Watching them perform with kids really gives you a sense of whether or not they have it. I always say, "You don't pay a pitcher a million dollars until you see him pitch."

11. Question: Is it important to you that teachers are willing to work over and above the demands of the classroom? Why?

Dr. Ancell: Yes, definitely, because I don't think the teaching job ends at the door to the classroom. A lot goes on outside, whether it be lesson preparation or student activities. That's an important part of the total picture. This willingness says that teaching is not just a job, it's a profession. This person has intrinsic motivation; they are not a clock puncher. To me it says you really care.

A PRINCIPAL'S PERSPECTIVE
Dr. Alice Quiocho
Alpine Union School District
Alpine, California

1. Question: How important do you think it is to have a teacher candidate acquaint him/herself with the school and district prior to the interview?

Dr. Quiocho: When you come into a school district, you enter a culture that is unique to the school community: the parents, students, teachers, and businesses. In order for a teacher to know how to best use his or her people skills, it is of vital importance that the teacher learn about the district, including who the important and influential people are, if possible.

2. Question: How important are the cover letter, the resumé, and the application?

Dr. Quiocho: The resumé and all its essential parts are important. They must be neat, not have any misspelled words, be well organized, address the posting, convey the teacher's voice and enthusiasm for kids and teaching.

3. Question: What are the most important characteristics of a teaching candidate?

Dr. Quiocho: The most important characteristics of a teacher candidate are: enthusiasm for kids

ability to communicate with a variety of people
willingness to grow professionally
flexibility
sense of humor
willingness to put in extra time to benefit children and the community
willingness to spend time communicating with parents about children in a positive manner
knowledge about instructional strategies
understanding about some research in teaching
knowledge about the reform/restructuring movement
knowledge about how to organize a classroom
knowledge about a discipline plan that works

4. Question: If a teacher candidate interviewed in this district and did not get the position, what would be your response if that person called for an appointment with you to discuss the interview and why he/she was not hired?

Dr. Quiocho: If a teacher was not hired, I would review the interview and the manner in which the teacher responded to the interview and compare that answer with what I felt was important for me at my school in terms of vision, curriculum, student needs, and parent needs. I would then suggest to the teacher candidate how he or she could improve in the next interview.

5. Question: Do you ever call former employers?

Dr. Quiocho: Yes, I always call former employers, because you do not get the "hidden" messages or comments about a teacher's performance in the application process.

6. Question: What are some suggestions you would offer a teacher candidate so that he/she might be more at ease during an interview?

Dr. Quiocho: Some advice I would offer is the following:

1. Know who you are and the things that you believe in.
2. Couple that knowledge with what you know about the community.
3. Look at the interview as a way to get to know key people in the district and let them get to know you.
4. Take time before you answer a question, and speak to the question. Only go beyond the question if you are asked to. It is not a problem to elaborate on something you have done, but do not go on and on. Watch the interviewers. If they shift around and lose eye contact with you, end your comments.
5. Make eye contact with **all** the panel members when you talk.

7. Question: What unspoken clues do you consider that might indicate to you whether or not a teacher candidate would be a good "match" with the community, a specific principal, a grade level, and/or subject area?

Dr. Quiocho: Paralinguistics is important to me. I look for those nonverbal clues such as tightening of the body when asked a question about staying late and putting in some extra time to serve kids. I listen for hesitation in the speech pattern and listen very closely to the tone of the voice. A sincere voice is full and vibrant and maintains an even tone with the proper emphasis. An insincere voice may crack and lose its intensity. Loss of eye contact is also a clue. When asked a difficult question, some candidates may lose eye contact. Sometimes, a candidate may answer a question too hastily with a "pat" answer (I've heard that before and quite often from insincere candidates), and that tells me that the candidate is telling me what I want to hear, or at least what he or she thinks I want to hear.

8. Question: All things being equal, do you ever make a decision for one candidate or another on a "gut level" feeling?

Dr. Quiocho: Yes, I have made a decision on a gut level feeling. I have thought long and hard about it, after checking references, and have gone with my gut feeling. I have not been wrong yet.

9. Question: Is it important to you that teachers are willing to work over and above the demands of the classroom? Why?

Dr. Quiocho: Absolutely. That gives the students and parents the message that the teachers care about their children. You see, when kids come to school, the parents feel that they have given us their best treasures. And, we as parents feel the same way. We want someone to love our children as much as we do, and the extra time and devotion is a clear message to parents and to me as the administrator.

A COUNSELOR'S COMMENTS
Sherrill K. Beck
Joan MacQueen Middle School
Alpine, California

I have been asked to comment on what traits I think are important and, in fact, necessary for a teacher to be effective in a classroom. Though there are probably many others that could be included, the following characteristics are essential for anyone teaching at any level in public education today.

The teacher

1. is aware of the students' unique cultural backgrounds;

2. constantly promotes positive re-inforcement;

3. really cares about each child he or she teaches;

4. is willing and able to be both organized and flexible;

5. meets each child at the learning level he/she has attained, building on the past and taking him/her forward "up and away" as far as possible;

6. is fair and consistent in behavior management and discipline;

7. relates learning to the child's current life and beyond;

8. is willing and eager to work with parents as part of the child's team of support;

9. understands the physical, psychological, emotional, and

10. is willing and able to try as many methods as are currently available to "reach and teach" individual students;

11. is a team player with other teachers and support staff at the school.

SUGGESTED READING LIST

Books

Atwell, Nancy, In the Middle

California State Department of Education, Caught in the Middle

Canter, Lee and Marlene, Assertive Discipline

Carnegie Council on Adolescent Development, Turning Points

Gollnick, Donna M., and Chin, Phillip C., Multicultural Education in a Pluralistic Society

Goodman, Ken, What's Whole in Whole Language

Heller, Mary, Reading-Writing Connections

Hunter, Madeline, Mastery Teaching (Clinical Teaching)

Johnson, David, Johnson, Roger, Johnson Holubec, Edith, and Roy, Patricia, Circles of Learning

The Report on the Commission on Reading, Becoming a Nation of Readers

SUGGESTED READING LIST

Piaget, Jean, and Inhelder, Bartel, <u>The Psychology of the Child</u>

Weaver, Constance, <u>Reading Process and Practice</u>

Willinsky, John, <u>The New Literacy</u>

Periodicals

"Educational Leadership" (K - 12)

"The English Journal" (Secondary)

"K - 8 Education"

"Language Arts" (K - 12)

"Learning Magazine" (K - 8)

"Phi Delta Kappan" (K - 12)

"Reading Teacher" (Elementary)

"Teacher Magazine" (K - 12)

For Additional Copies of

HOW TO GET THE TEACHING POSITION YOU WANT!

Please clearly print your first and last name and complete address, including ZIP code. Send $19.95 for *each* copy (includes tax and shipping),
($24.95 in Canada)
to:

EDUCATIONAL ENTERPRISES
P.O. Box 1836
Spring Valley, CA 91979

.BE PREPARED

.BE PROFESSIONAL

.BE SUCCESSFUL